UNSILENCED

UNSILENCED

A Journey of Breaking Cycles, Healing Trauma and Rewriting My Story

Shalara Webb

Unsilenced
A Journey of Breaking Cycles, Healing Trauma and Rewriting My Story

ISBNs:
979-8-234-08951-9 (hardback)
979-8-234-12183-7 (paperback)

Contents

Acknowledgments

First and foremost, I give all honor and thanks to God for carrying me through every season of my life and giving me the strength to tell my story.

I would like to express my sincere gratitude to my Book Coach Carita Montgomery and her incredible team for their guidance, encouragement, patience, and unwavering support throughout this journey. Your expertise and belief in my voice helped bring this book to life in a way I never imagined possible.

A very special thank you to my Aunt Liz for connecting me with the right people at the right time. What began as a simple conversation turned into the fulfillment of a dream, and I will forever be grateful for that divine connection.

To my children Quintil, Rashantta, Javarus, Cheron, Lira and my grandchildren, thank you for being my reason, my motivation, and my greatest blessings. Every lesson, every sacrifice, every tear, and every triumph has been tied to the love I have for you. This book would not exist without you.

To My Love and Best Friend Danny, thank you for continuously encouraging me, believing in me, and pushing me to complete this journey even during the moments I wanted to give up. Your support has meant more than words could ever express.

To my support group, the "1 Best Committee," and to my family and friends — thank you for your prayers, encouragement, love, and support throughout the years. Your presence in my life has helped shape my healing journey.

And finally, to my parents, Juanita and Willie Webb — though you are no longer here physically, I feel your love surrounding me every day. I pray that I have made you proud. Your lives, your love, and even your absence helped shape the woman I became.

Preface

In a perfect world…a child is born into a home with two married parents—both present, both loving, both guiding. That was always my desire for my children. But life doesn't always follow perfect plan and if I've learned anything…it's that love, parenting, and purpose don't always come wrapped in perfection. So, before you read my story…I want to begin with something honest. Something vulnerable. Something necessary. This is an open apology.

To my children. I'm sorry. Not because I didn't love you. But because I didn't always know how to love you in the healthiest way. I grew up without my parents. My mother and father both passed away when I was very young. So, before I ever became a mother…I was already learning life through loss. Through absence. Through questions that never got answered. And because of that…I made a promise to myself.

My children would never experience life without both parents. But life doesn't just respond to promises. It responds to choices. And some of the choices I made as a teenager…and as a young adult…did not lead me in the direction I truly desired. Not because I didn't have options. But because

I didn't always have clarity. Some of my decisions came from rebellion. Some came from pain. Some came from trying to figure life out without the guidance I needed. Because when you're young you believe you know everything. And life has a way of humbling that belief. So, this apology is not rooted in shame. It's rooted in awareness. Because I now understand that my upbringing...the silence I was taught...the environment I navigated...all played a role in how I showed up as a parent.

In my generation, children didn't have a voice. What adults said... was final.

And you learned very quickly not to question it. So many of us learned to be quiet. To suppress.

To endure. And when you grow up that way you don't always realize the damage it causes. Because silence doesn't heal pain. It hides it. And hidden pain...doesn't disappear. It shows up later. For a long time, I didn't understand that. And because of that I didn't always allow my children the space to express themselves freely. For that...I am sorry.

It wasn't until my youngest child came along that something began to shift in me. I watched her express herself openly and it challenged me. It made me reflect. Because I realized something important: Listening is not weakness. Understanding is not disrespect. My older children sometimes say, "You've gotten soft. "But what they don't see is this: I didn't get soft. I became aware.

Life taught me the importance of mental and emotional health. Something we didn't talk about growing up. We were taught to be strong. But many of us were just hurting. We just didn't know how to process it. So, it came out in other ways. Even now, I still reflect on my parents.

My mother, I remember seeing her in her casket. My father, I remember his love. His presence. He showed up and that matters. Because parenting is about presence. I remember him taking us to the airport just to watch planes take off. And later in life I faced my fears and got on a plane. And I felt peace, so thank you, Dad.

To my children and to you reading this we will make mistakes. But the goal is growth. The goal is awareness. The goal is being willing to say: "I could have done better... and now I will." Because parenting is not defined by perfection. It is defined by unconditional love and love requires growth. Every day we wake up we get another chance. Another chance to heal. Another chance to grow. Another chance to rewrite our story. And this book...is part of mine.

Chapter 1

Innocence Interrupted

Before life teaches you what loss really is...you believe you have time.

Time to grow up. Time to ask questions. Time to understand your parents... and be understood by them. But what happens when time is taken before you even know how to ask for it?

I know... because I was that child. As a little girl, I lived in my imagination. I would sit quietly and daydream—not about toys or games—but about what my life could have been. I imagined a different version of my world. A version where things didn't feel so incomplete.

Not that I knew exactly what I was missing. I just felt it. A void. A silence where answers should have been. Because the truth is—I never had a chance. A chance to fully get to know my parents. A chance to experience them as I grew up. A chance to understand what life could have been with them. That absence became the loudest presence in my life. My mother passed away at just 24 years old from breast cancer. I was too young to understand what that meant. I remember sitting in the back of a church… watching, listening, but not truly grasping what was happening. I didn't understand death. I didn't understand finality.

I only knew something had changed. And nothing felt the same.

Years later, my father passed away.

But his story came with silence… secrets… and shame that didn't belong to me.

I didn't learn the truth the way a child should—through love and honesty.

I found out by accident. One day, my aunt asked me to grab something from her purse. Inside, I saw a document with my father's name on it. That's when I learned the truth about his diagnosis. HIV.

Yes… HIV. And I say it out loud now—because back then, I wasn't allowed to.

I remember being in school, a discussion topic on HIV. I shared that my father passed away from pneumonia due to complications from HIV. I spoke honestly.

I said what my father passed away from. And instead of being comforted… I was corrected. Silenced. Made to feel like I had done something wrong. Imagine being a child… grieving… confused…and then being told your truth is something to hide.

That moment taught me something early: "Don't say too much." "Don't feel too openly." "Don't make people uncomfortable with your truth." And that stayed with me.

Adults often say they are protecting children. But I've asked myself over and over again: Who are you really protecting? Because from where I stood it didn't feel like protection.

It felt like isolation. Even in the midst of loss, there were small pockets of love that stayed with me.

My grandmother. She had quiet strength about her. People said she looked mean—but she was gentle with me. She talked to her plants like they were people. And I thought she was the strangest woman in the world. But those plants? They thrived. And so did I… when I was with her. I Remember the smell of her home of moth balls she kept in her drawers.… the sweetness of peanut brittle she'd share… the comfort of simply being seen. Her house felt like stability. Like something I could hold onto.

And then… she was gone too.

Another loss. Another shift. Another piece of my world taken.

If you can, picture this: A little girl. Trying to understand why the people who loved her keep disappearing. First her mother. Then her grandmother. Then her father. Three losses. Before she even reached middle school. That kind of grief doesn't just pass.

It settles. It shapes how you see life. How you trust. How you love. How you protect yourself.

When my father was alive, I watched him change. From strong… to fragile. From present… to fading. But no one explained what was happening. No one prepared me. And to this day, I carry a quiet resentment—not out of anger… but out of longing. Because I often wonder: What if I knew? Would I have loved him louder? Would I have stayed a little longer during visits? Would I have said more? After he passed, everything changed again. My brother and I went to live with my aunt. And while she stepped in—and I am grateful for that—it was different.

Because no matter how much someone tries…you can feel the difference when it's not your parent. That's not to blame. That's truth. Life shifted again—from a home where my father worked hard to provide…back into an environment that felt unfamiliar and unstable. She did her best. She made sure I had nice clothes. We celebrated birthdays. She provided what she knew how to give. But emotionally… things were different. Discipline was different as we were corrected but also taught manners. Even being brought up on chores with cleaning and dusting every Saturday morning..

Love felt different. And as a child, you don't always have the words for that. You just feel it.

Now as a woman... as a mother... I understand something I didn't then: People raise you from what they know. From what they were taught. From what they survived.

And sometimes... that means cycles continue without question. But here's where my story begins to shift. Because even in all that loss... confusion... silence...Something inside of me was waking up.

A quiet awareness. A realization that said: "This doesn't have to continue." This is where the cycle meets a decision. And that decision is this: I will not repeat what broke me. This chapter is not just about loss. It's about awareness. Because before you can have clarity...before you can find peace...before you can walk in freedom...You have to acknowledge where it all began.

And for me...It began with innocence interrupted.

The loss of my parents and grandmother created wounds I carried long before I understood grief. Looking back, I realize that many of my struggles began with the unanswered questions and emotional void left behind by those losses. This chapter reminds us that childhood trauma does not disappear simply because we grow older it follows us until we choose to heal.

Chapter 2
The First Trauma

There are some things you don't realize were trauma…because they looked like everyday life.

In the late 80s, the crack epidemic didn't just exist—it lived in our neighborhoods. It was everywhere. On the corners. In conversations. In households. In people you know and people you love. Either someone was using it…or someone was selling it. And as a child, you don't analyze it. You absorb it. For me, it became normal. Fights in the streets. Police raids.

People walking by… lost in addiction.

It was like watching a show that never turned off. And nothing about it felt shocking.

It just was. When dysfunction is consistent…it starts feeling familiar. At the same time, I was shifting internally. Trying to process emotions I didn't have words for. Still carrying the loss of my father…still feeling a void that never quite filled. You learn to function. You show up.

You smile. You do what's expected. But inside, there are moments. Moments where you cry.

Moments where you feel overwhelmed. I was raised in what was familiar...not always what was healthy. My Aunt eventually moved us in a house out of that environment.

People say I grew up too fast. But it wasn't that. It was exposure. When you see too much too soon...you think you understand life. But really, you're learning survival. And for many girls like me...this was normal. That's where love gets confusing. Attention feels like love.

Familiarity feels like safety.

I found my escape in cheerleading. It gave me structure. Focus. Identity. But it also gave me attention. And I later learned...all attention is not good attention. I would still find myself shutting down. Sitting quietly. Observing. Avoiding my emotions. Then life shifted again.

An incident changed everything.

My sibling and I moved in with my grandfather. And it was hard. I felt like he treated me differently. The boys were praised. But me...I felt unseen. We moved back into my father's home. But it didn't feel like home anymore. It felt like loss. I was afraid.

So I coped the only way I knew how. I distracted myself. I avoided the pain.

Some may say it was my fault. But I was just a kid. Trying to understand a world that kept changing. Trying to find love. Trying to survive. This is where awareness begins. Because before clarity...there's confusion. Before peace...there's survival. Before freedom there's awareness. And this was the beginning of mine.

Growing up in an environment where dysfunction became normal taught me how easily we can mistake survival for living. What I once accepted as everyday life was shaping my beliefs about love, safety, and self-worth. Healing began when I learned that what is familiar is not always healthy.

Chapter 3

Growing Up Too Fast

Some moments in life don't just change your direction...they change who you have to become.

I became a mother at 14. Even saying that now, as a grown woman, it still feels heavy. Because at 14, you're still trying to figure yourself out. And I didn't even know I was pregnant at first. When my family found out, everything moved fast. Decisions were being made.

Conversations were being had. Plans were being put in place. And none of them included asking me how I felt.

To be fair, I was a child. And as I look back now, I understand why they responded the way they did. But understanding that now doesn't erase what it felt like then. Because in that moment, I wasn't thinking about long-term consequences. I was thinking like a 14-year-old girl. They took me to a clinic. The plan was for me to have an abortion. But I was further along than they realized. And something shifted. My grandmother was against it. And it was in that moment I learned something else: My mother had also been a young mother. I was standing in the middle of a cycle that I didn't even know existed.

Emotionally, I didn't fully understand what was happening. Part of me was scared.

Part of me was confused. And part of me was living in a fairytale. Because I thought I knew what motherhood looked like. But there's a difference between playing a role and living a reality. At the same time, something else was happening. Whispers. Judgment. Shame.

I had already been raised in church. But now, it felt different. I was being examined. Being pulled to the altar. People praying over me. Looking at me as if I had done something unforgivable. And I remember thinking: Did anyone stop to ask how I feel? Because yes, I was a young girl. But I was still a person. Instead, I felt labeled. I felt watched. I felt talked about.

So I started shrinking. I started pulling back. I wanted to disappear when I walked into rooms. And then another truth surfaced. I found out about SSI. Money had been coming in for me.

And that changed how I saw everything.

Because for so long, I had been made to feel like a burden. Now I questioned everything. With my pregnancy, I had to leave my regular school. I was placed in a school for girls who were pregnant. At first, it felt like separation. But in hindsight, it became a blessing. Because for the first time, I wasn't alone. I was surrounded by girls who understood. That school allowed us to continue learning. And I held onto that. I made sure my grades stayed up. But there was still loss. I had to give up cheerleading. And that was my escape. At the same time, I was trying to understand that I had a life growing inside of me. And something in me knew I had to grow up fast. But mentally, I was still a child.

Looking back now, I see it clearly. And as I became a mother, a new fear entered my life. Not for me, but for my daughter. I didn't want her to repeat my story. Because once you've lived it, you see it differently. This chapter is about what happens when innocence meets responsibility too soon. And how awareness becomes the beginning of change.

Becoming a mother at fourteen changed the course of my life forever. Although I was judged by many, that experience taught me resilience, responsibility, and determination. Looking back, I see a young girl doing her best while carrying burdens she was never prepared to carry.

Chapter 4

Change of Course

Sometimes life doesn't ask you what you want…It just moves you. After my daughter was born, everything shifted again. When I left the hospital, I went to live with my mother's oldest sister. Through family circumstances and decisions that were bigger than me, she legally adopted me.

I am grateful. Because she didn't have to do it. She had her own life, her own children, her own responsibilities. And yet, she made space for me and my daughter. But gratitude and emotion can exist at the same time. Because while I was thankful, I was also torn.

Part of me was excited. I had always imagined what it would be like to be with my mother's side of the family. But the other part of me was grieving. Because I was leaving behind my brother, my cousins, and my familiar world. I remember thinking, why can't I have it all?

Living with my aunt was different. In her eyes, I was still a child. But I wasn't just a child anymore. I was a child with a child. And that changes something inside of you.

When it came to my daughter, my aunt stepped in fully. She took control, handled things, and made decisions. And instead of stepping into responsibility, I stepped back. I continued living like a teenager. Going to school, getting back into cheer, focusing on what still made me feel like me. But internally, something was off. Because while everyone saw me as a young girl, I didn't feel like one. I felt caught between two identities. Too grown to be just a child. Too unprepared to fully be a woman.

When people saw me with my daughter, the comments came. She's just a baby having a baby.

She's too young. And those words stayed with me. Sometimes I felt relieved when people thought my daughter was my aunt's. Because I didn't have to carry the judgment. But reality caught up. One day, my aunt asked me to do something for my daughter. And I didn't do it. That's when everything changed. My aunt put her foot down. And I had to quit cheerleading.

That moment broke me. Because cheer was my escape, my identity, my joy. So I rebelled.

I stopped caring. I acted out. Because it felt like something had been taken from me again. Looking back now, I can see both sides. I was a young girl reacting from emotion and my aunt was trying to teach responsibility. My daughter was my responsibility. And my aunt knew how to get my attention. She removed what I valued most. She wasn't trying to hurt me. She was trying to prepare me. But the little girl she thought she was raising was already gone. Life had already changed me. This chapter is about identity. About being forced to grow up before you're ready. About wanting to be understood while still trying to understand yourself. I was a young girl trying to hold onto pieces of myself while life kept demanding more. This was my change of course.

Moving into a new home gave me opportunities, but it also brought new challenges and expectations. During this season, I struggled between wanting freedom and accepting responsibility. Sometimes the people who love us most make difficult decisions that we only understand years later.

Chapter 5

A Child Becoming a Wife

There are decisions you make in life...and then there are decisions you feel like life makes for you. By the end of my junior year in high school...I found myself pregnant again. And this time...it hit different. It wasn't planned. It wasn't expected. And honestly, because Of how my body worked, I didn't realize how fast I could become pregnant.. But there I was. Standing at another crossroads.

Senior year was ahead of me. Plans were in motion. I was part of HOSA—Health Occupation Students of America. I had dreams. Real dreams. I wanted to be in the medical field.

I wanted to become a pediatrician. I wasn't just surviving anymore...I was starting to see a future. And then...everything paused. Because now the conversation wasn't about my dreams.

It was about my decisions. In my family, having children out of wedlock carried weight. Expectation. Judgment. Concern about my future. And once again...an ultimatum was placed in front of me.

This time...I chose to have an abortion. And I need to say this plainly: That decision broke something in me. Because while it may have made sense to everyone else...emotionally...I wasn't prepared for what came after. I will never forget that moment. The ultrasound.

Seeing my child. My baby's head turned to the side...as if they were posing. That image never left me. And no one prepared me for that part. I went into a depression. A deep one.

And instead of healing...I went back into what I knew. I rebelled. Again, as my boyfriend at the time asked for another kid.

And before I could even process what I had just been through...I found myself pregnant...again.

And this time...there was no room for discussion. My aunt was firm. There would be no more children in her house. And the solution? Marriage.

At 16 years old...I became a wife. And if I'm honest...I didn't fully understand what that meant.

Part of me thought I was stepping into freedom. But freedom without understanding...is just another form of bondage. Because the very next day...I cried.

Reality hit. The excitement was gone. It felt heavy. Permanent. I remember thinking: Can I go back? But I couldn't. And just like that...I had to grow up. I had no parents to fall back on.

My guardians were disappointed. Some family still supported me... but for the most part...I was on my own. But even in that...I didn't give up completely. I went back to school.

Back to the school for pregnant girls. But this time...I was a wife. A mother. And pregnant again. And somehow...I still finished. I graduated. Nine months pregnant... walking across that stage...and the entire room stood up. That moment meant everything. Because I knew what people had said. But I did it. But here's the truth I had to face later: I didn't keep going. Not because I wasn't capable. But because I allowed the voices around me...to become louder than the voice within me.

So, I stepped into survival. I worked. I provided. I showed up. Because quitting...was no longer an option. I had two little lives depending on me. This chapter isn't just about marriage. It's about pressure. Pain. And decisions made before healing. It's about understanding that purpose doesn't disappear. It waits. And even though I didn't know it then...my story wasn't over. It was just taking another turn.

At sixteen, I thought marriage would solve my problems and make me grown. Instead, it taught me that adulthood is much more than age or legal status. Major life decisions made from fear, pressure, or immaturity often carry consequences that shape our future.

Chapter 6

The Reality of Becoming a Mother

At some point life stops asking if you're ready. And for me that moment came when I looked around and realized there were little eyes watching me. Depending on me. Whether I felt ready or not I didn't have a choice anymore. I was a mother.

So I did what I knew how to do. I worked.

Getting a job wasn't foreign to me. Responsibility wasn't foreign to me. So I worked and, in my mind, I believed I was doing the best I could. Did I struggle? Yes. But my children didn't feel it the way I did. They had what they needed. The basics. Food. Clothes. Shelter. And what I didn't realize then was that while I was raising them. I was also raising myself. I grew up with my children. And it was hard.

Motherhood didn't come with a manual. So, I parented from what I knew. "What I say goes." Looking back now I see where I didn't give them a voice. Not because I didn't love them but because I didn't know how.

Motherhood is learning in real time. Every decision I made I believed it was right. Would I do some things differently now? Yes. But I did what I knew.

And I will never regret my children. They are all blessings.

There was a time I lost a pregnancy. And that pain was deep. But even in that God met me.

Later, I had my youngest daughter. And during her birth I was afraid. But she made it.

She was fine.

And I felt relief like never before. Motherhood will stretch you. You need God. Because motherhood requires strength you don't naturally have. And it doesn't get easier. It changes.

There are no days off. No quitting. When you are a mother, you stand. You protect. You show up. Even now I'm still there for my children. And I'm grateful. Because my mother didn't get this chance.

My prayer has always been "God, please let my children become adults before you take me". Because I never wanted them to feel what I felt. Motherhood isn't about being perfect. It's about being present and choosing every day to grow.

Motherhood became my greatest responsibility and one of my greatest teachers. While I made mistakes, I also learned valuable lessons about sacrifice, unconditional love, and perseverance. My children grew up with me, and together we learned how to navigate life one day at a time.

Chapter 7
Love or Control

When you're young do you really know what love is? Or do you just know what you've seen?

What you've felt, what you've been taught or what you've survived?

For a long time, I thought I knew what love looked like. But what I really knew was what I was exposed to. Behind closed doors love didn't always look gentle. It looked like arguments. Raised voices. Harsh words. Sometimes even hands being laid where they shouldn't be.

And then just as quickly as it started it would end. Apologies. Laughter. Cuddling. Like nothing ever happened and when you grow up seeing that you begin to normalize it. You begin to believe: "This is just how love is." So, when you enter relationships, you don't question it. You repeat it. You think love is: "We fight then we make up." You think passion equals intensity.

You think chaos equals connection. But what no one teaches you is this: That's not love.

That's a cycle. And cycles feel familiar. Even when they're unhealthy.

There were moments I thought love meant being checked on constantly. Having to explain where I was. Who I was with. When I will be back. And instead of seeing it for what it was I told myself: "He cares about me." But over time I realized something deeper. Control can look like care until it starts taking your voice. And when you've never fully had a voice, you don't always recognize when it's being taken.

There were times when alcohol played a role. Excuses were made. "It was the alcohol."

"I didn't mean it." "I blacked out and I accepted it. Because again it felt familiar. But familiarity doesn't equal healthy. It wasn't until I began to see something different that I started questioning everything. I saw that disagreement didn't have to mean destruction.

That communication didn't have to turn into conflict. That love didn't have to hurt.

I saw that two people could disagree and still respect each other. Still pause. Still choose peace. And that shifted something in me.

Because I knew something about myself: My words could cut deep. I could say things in the heat of a moment that I couldn't take back. And after the moment passed there was no satisfaction in "winning." Just damage. And when children are watching that damage doesn't stay between two people. It spreads. Because what they see they learn. And what they learn... they repeat. That's how cycles continue. For a long time I made excuses.

"It's just how I was raised."

"It's just where I come from."

"This is how relationships are."

But at some point you have to pause and ask yourself: "Is this really what I want my life to feel like?" Because love, real love doesn't leave you feeling trapped. It doesn't silence you. It doesn't make you feel like you're walking on eggshells. Love is peace. And peace doesn't mean perfect. It means safe. It means heard. It means respected.

As I grew, I started to change. Not overnight. But little by little. I started thinking differently.

Responding differently. Choosing differently. Because I had children watching me. And I didn't want them to grow up thinking this is what love looks like. So, I had to unlearn. Unlearning the fighting. Unlearn the reacting. Unlearn the need to "win." And learn something new. That love doesn't harm. That love doesn't control. That love doesn't take your voice.

And while I'm still growing still learning one thing I know for sure is this: If it costs you your peace it's not love.

This chapter isn't just about relationships. It's about awareness. It's about recognizing the difference between what feels familiar and what is actually healthy. Because once you know the difference you can choose differently. And that choice can change everything.

For many years, I confused control, chaos, and dysfunction with love because those patterns felt familiar. Real love should bring peace, not fear. Healthy relationships are built on respect, trust, communication, and emotional safety.

Chapter 8
Consequences

Sometime life changes in a moment you never saw coming. I remember being at work one day, talking with a coworker that was someone I considered a good friend. We were just having a regular conversation and somehow the topic came up about someone going to jail. And I remember saying something so casually… "That could never be me."

That very night my life changed. I was asleep on the couch. My baby boy was only two years old. The phone rang. There was chaos on the other end. I didn't think. I just ran. When I got outside, I saw my husband. Something didn't feel right. He told me to take a firearm into the house. I didn't like guns. I didn't deal with guns. But at that moment, I reacted. It was placed on my shirt, ran inside, and tossed it on the couch. When I turned around police were everywhere. Lights. Guns drawn and suddenly…I was the one being shouted at. "Put your hands up!" I remember thinking: What did I do?

Within seconds, I was on the ground. My children were inside the house crying and watching.

Before they took me away, an officer said: "This night could have gone a whole different way."

That stayed with me. I was taken to the station. Handcuffed. Confused. Asking myself over and over: What did I do?

Then I found out and I couldn't believe it. Something so small had turned into something so big.

I spent the night in jail. Afraid. Lost. The next day, I was transferred. Because now it was a felony. And I thought: How did my life get here? I bonded out. But it didn't end there. Court dates. Fear. Pressure. I took a plea. Not because I fully understood but because I was afraid. Five years' probation. And just like that my life shifted again.

I followed every rule. Did everything I was supposed to do. And eventually…it was dismissed. I remember running out of that courtroom thanking God.

But even after that the question remained: Have you ever been arrested? And I had to answer over and over again. Until one day someone believed me. And that moment mattered. Because I had been carrying something heavy. What I learned is this: It only takes one moment…one decision… to change your life. People will always say what they would have done.

But the truth is you don't know until you're in it.

This chapter is about consequences. About understanding that every decision carries weight.

And about giving grace. Because not everyone who gets arrested…is a criminal. Sometimes…it's just a moment changed everything.

One split-second decision changed the trajectory of my life. The experience taught me that circumstances are not always what they appear to be and that judgment often comes long before understanding. It also taught me the importance of standing in your truth.

Chapter 9

Losing Myself

You can become so consumed with life that you don't even realize you're disappearing in it.

Day after day you wake up. You take care of everyone. You show up. You handle what needs to be handled and somewhere in the middle of all of that…you forget about you.

People will say, "You're so strong." But what they don't see is this: Sometimes I felt weak.

Sometimes I didn't want to fight anymore. But life doesn't stop just because you're tired.

So I kept going. But something inside of me shifted. I felt different. Sad…heavy…and I couldn't explain why. So, I went to a psychiatrist.

I didn't tell anyone because I didn't want people to think I was crazy. That's how we were raised. She told me I was depressed. And for the first time…there was a name for what I felt.

She gave me medication. But when I told my aunt, she told me not to take it. So, I didn't.

And I was stuck again. Knowing something was wrong but not knowing what to do. Life kept moving. But I wasn't living. I was surviving. I remember hearing my daughter called me "hell on wheels." That hurt. But I knew I was angry. Angry about my life. Angry about what I was carrying. And instead of dealing with it…I kept going.

I leaned on my cousin. She was my safe place. But even that became too much.

Because I kept going back to the same situation. So, I stopped talking. And I started carrying everything alone. That's when I became numb. Still smiling. Still showing up. But empty.

What people saw was not the real me. It was survival. I didn't want judgment. I didn't want "I told you so." So, I pretended. The only place I felt peace was with my grandmother.

Being around her felt like being close to my mother. But when she passed…I lost that too. I would go to her grave. Sit there. Cry. Talk. Trying to feel something again. But my depression got worse. I didn't even realize it because I got used to feeling that way.

One night…I cried out to God. "Why are you letting this happen to me?" And I heard clearly: "I gave you a way out." And I knew it was true. But I kept going back.

Because what's familiar can feel safer than what's unknown. Even when it hurts you.

I started losing my sense of worth. Believing things about myself that weren't true.

That I wasn't enough. That no one would want me. That's what emotional pain does.

It changes how you see yourself. I tried to cope. Shopping. Hair. Nails. Smiling on the outside.

But dying on the inside.

Until one day...after everything ended...I smiled. And it was real. And I realized...I had lost myself. Trying to make everyone else happy. Trying to survive. But I also realized this: You can find yourself again. This chapter is about losing yourself quietly. And understanding...just because you're functioning...doesn't mean you're whole.

Healing begins when you admit: "I am not okay." And give yourself permission to become whole again.

You can spend so much time taking care of everyone else that you forget who you are. Depression often hides behind smiles, responsibilities, and routines. Healing begins when we acknowledge our pain instead of pretending it doesn't exist.

Chapter 10
Breaking Free

Sometimes your breaking point doesn't come from one moment. It comes from a realization.

For me, it started with a conversation. My uncle, one of my favorites, the one who always had stories, always kept it real and began talking about his life. What he saw growing up, what our family had experienced. And something clicked. It wasn't just a story anymore. It was a pattern. I began to see it clearly. My grandmother went through it. My mother went through it. And now...I was living it.

And in that moment, I said to myself: "No... not me. Not again." That was the first time I truly recognized it: A generational cycle. And something in me shifted. Because now it wasn't just about me. It was about my daughters. I started seeing things differently. Watching them.

Listening to them. Even noticing how they were navigating relationships. And I saw glimpses of the same patterns. The same confusion. The same dysfunction. And I knew right then: "I have to do better. I have to show them better."

That was the moment I decided I was choosing me. For the first time. I stopped making excuses. Stopped sitting out of life. Stopped shrinking myself to fit into something that was already breaking me. Even something as simple as going out with my cousins...became a statement. Because for so long, I didn't go anywhere. Didn't do anything.

Didn't allow myself to live. And I had convinced myself that was normal.

But it wasn't.

Then came the moment that confirmed everything I already felt. One day, I was on social media. Something I had been discouraged from even having. And as I scrolled...I came across a name. A name I had heard before. Something in my spirit paused. So, I looked. And what I found... shifted everything. A child. Not just any child. A child connected to my husband. And in that moment...everything went still.

Not because I didn't suspect things before. There had been cheating. Rumors. Situations. But this made it real. And I remember thinking: "What am I going to do now?" Because at that point I had just had my youngest. I was tired. Overwhelmed. Already stretched thin. And now...this? I tried to process it logically. Tried to plan. "I'll stay until my baby gets older. "I'll wait until things are easier." But here's what I learned: When you're done... you're done. And no plan can hold you in a place you've already outgrown.

Because deep down...I knew it was over. Not just the situation. But the version of me that kept accepting it. And another truth hit me hard: I couldn't embrace that situation in a healthy way.

Not because I lacked compassion. But because I knew my limits. I knew what I had experienced. I knew what I carried. And I refused to allow another child to feel what I had seen before rejection. Division. Distance.

So instead of forcing something that wasn't real…I chose honesty with myself. And that honesty said: "You can't stay here anymore." That was my breaking point. Not out of anger. Not out of revenge. But out of clarity.

And sometimes…clarity is the most powerful thing you can have. Because once you see something clearly…you can't unsee it.

And once you know your worth… you can't keep settling. Breaking free didn't happen the way I planned. But it happened the way it needed to. Because for the first time…I wasn't choosing survival. I was choosing myself. This chapter isn't just about leaving a relationship.

It's about breaking cycles. It's about recognizing patterns that no longer serve you.

And making a decision…that your story will not end the same way it started.

Because healing begins…when you finally say: "This stops with me."

Breaking generational cycles requires courage because it often means choosing a path no one around you has chosen before. Freedom begins the moment we stop accepting what hurts us as normal. Sometimes loving yourself means having the courage to walk away.

Chapter 11

The Turning Point

Sometimes your life doesn't change all at once…it changes when something inside of you finally says" Enough." After everything…I told myself I was going to live. Not just survive. But live.

I started going out with my cousins. Laughing again. Breathing again. And somewhere in that space…I met someone. Not a relationship. Not anything complicated. Just a friend.

But sometimes…God will send people into your life not to stay but to wake you up.

We talked. Shared life. Shared struggles. And one day, I said something about myself, something negative. Something I had started to believe.

And he stopped me. "What are you talking about? You're beautiful." And in that moment…something shifted. Because when you've been told the opposite long enough…you start to believe it. You question yourself. Your worth. Your value. Your beauty.

And I didn't realize how much I had shrunk myself...until someone reflected something different back to me.

That was the beginning. Not the end. Because even though I knew I was done...life still had one more moment for me. One more test. One more confirmation.

There was another altercation. And I remember sitting at a stoplight talking to God.

"God, I'm going to fight...but this is the last time." "If you get me through this...I'm done." And that moment came. And I kept my word. I was done.

Not halfway done. Not "thinking about it" done. Done.

And even when people tried to pull me back...to fix it...to reset it...to start over...I had already made my decision. Because when peace hits you...real peace...you don't question it. You protect it. And that's what I felt.

Peace. But healing...doesn't always come quietly. Sometimes it comes with anger.

Because now...you see everything clearly. The manipulation. The control.

The fear tactics. And you realize—you allowed it. And that realization...can make you angry. But even that anger...was part of my healing. Because it led me to a moment...that changed everything.

I was at work one day. And I told my boss someone who had known me for years "My chest hurts." She looked at me and said, "How long?" I said..."A week." And in that moment...everything got real. I drove myself to the hospital. And what I thought was just stress...was something much bigger. My blood pressure...was out of control. Dangerously high.

Room to room...test after test...until they finally said: "You're going to ICU."

And I remember thinking... "How did I get here? But the truth was...I already knew.

Stress. Pain. Holding everything in. And then...it dropped. Too low. And in that moment...I thought about my grandmother. I remembered watching her take her last breath.

And fear hit me. "I don't want to die." "I'm not ready." "I have to fight."

And I did.

I fought my way out of that bed. And when I came out of ICU...I came out different. Because now I understood something clearly: If I didn't change my life...my life would end. I was diagnosed with severe hypertension. And while doctors gave me medication...I knew the root. My emotions. My environment. My stress.

So the question became: "What are you going to do about it?"

Because healing requires action.

And one day...my cousin said something that changed everything: "You have a chance to rewrite your story." And just like that...it clicked. For the first time in a long time...I was free.

Free to choose. Free to move. Free to live. And I refused to go back.

Even when it was hard. Even when it was scary. Even when I didn't know what was next.

I chose me. And that choice...saved my life.

This chapter isn't just about a turning point. It's about a decision.

The moment you stop waiting...and start choosing yourself.

Because sometimes...your life doesn't change until you do.

My health crisis forced me to face the reality that emotional pain affects the body as much as the mind. This chapter marks the moment I stopped surviving and started choosing myself. Sometimes God allows disruption because He is preparing us for transformation.

Chapter 12
Facing Myself

For a while, it looked like I had finally started living. I was outside. Traveling. Laughing again. My girl cousins on my mom's side kept me moving, kept me busy, kept me distracted. And honestly, I needed that. Because in the middle of a divorce, sometimes movement feels like healing. Sometimes noise feels like peace. But noise doesn't last forever.

Life started shifting. Jobs changed. Schedules changed. Promotions came. Responsibilities grew. And just like that… the outings slowed down. The calls weren't as frequent. The distractions got quiet. And that's when it hit me. Silence. Not the peaceful kind. The kind that forces you to sit with yourself. That's when I had to ask a question I had been avoiding my entire life: "What do you want?" Not what the marriage needed. Not what the kids needed. Not what survival required. Me. And the truth? I didn't know. I had spent so many years being a wife, being a mother, being everything to everybody else… that I had no idea who I was outside of that. So when the kids went off for visitation… when some had already moved out… when the house got quiet… It was just me. And I didn't know what to do with that. That kind of emptiness will creep up on you. It doesn't kick the door in—it whispers. It makes you question everything. It made me question everything. "Am I going to be alone?" "Was everything they said about me true?" "Am I too old now?" "Will anybody really want me?" Even though I wasn't looking for a relationship, I still had a friend—someone I talked to, someone who lived in another state. It was light. It was fun. But it wasn't real life. And deep down, I knew that. Because at night… when everything settled… it was just me and my thoughts. And those thoughts were loud.

I started replaying everything. The marriage. The choices. The years I stayed. And I had to ask myself the hard question: "What was I really fighting for?" Because here's the truth nobody likes to say out loud: You can love someone… You can mean your vows… You can try your hardest… And still be in something that's broken beyond repair. I won't say my marriage was all bad. It wasn't. But I will say this: When the damage outweighs the good…When you're constantly in survival mode…When peace feels like a stranger… That's not love. That's endurance. And I was tired of enduring. People can say what they want. They can judge. They can question why you stayed or why you left. But they weren't living it. I was.And I know I was a good wife. I believed in my vows. I gave my all. I stayed until I knew—I mean really knew—I was done.

But now, I had to be honest about something else too. Maybe I stayed longer than I should have… because I was holding on to what I thought marriage was supposed to be. "You married, you stay. You stick it out. No matter what." But what if it was never built the right way to begin with? Because if I'm being completely honest…That marriage started from a pregnancy. And when you're young… do you really know what love is?

Not fully. You can grow into love, yes. I believe that. But if the foundation is cracked from the start… it makes everything else harder. And I think deep down, I always knew that. I kept hoping things would change. That he would grow. That we would grow. But one thing my auntie—my mama's oldest sister, the one who adopted me—told me stuck with me forever: "Baby… a leopard don't change their spots. They just find new ways to do things."

I didn't understand it then. But I understand it now. And not just about him… but about me too. Because change doesn't happen just because time passes. Change happens when you decide to look in the mirror and deal with what you see. And I had to do that. I had to face me Not him.

Not the past. Me. I had to admit that I had become bitter. Angry. Guarded. And I didn't want to live like that anymore. That wasn't who I was. I wanted to laugh again. For real. I wanted peace. For real. I wanted joy that didn't come from distractions. So, I had to start doing the hardest work of all: Taking accountability. Not blame. Accountability. Looking at my role. My patterns. The things I allowed. The things I ignored. And asking myself: "How do I become better?"

Because one thing I knew for sure…I didn't want to carry this version of me into anything new. There was a point where I said I was done with love completely. "I'm just going to be by myself. Forever." And I meant it. Because I was tired. Tired of being hurt. Tired of giving my all just to feel broken in return. But deep down… I also knew that wasn't the life God had for me. I knew I was meant to love again. To be loved again. To be a wife again. But not like before. Better. Healthier. Stronger. And that meant I had work to do. Real work. Because one thing about me? I hold on. I hold on to pain. I hold on to hurt. I hold on to memories long after they should've been released. And that comes from everything I've been through.

Because when you've given your all... When you've been genuine... When you've been loyal... And somebody breaks you to your core...It does something to you. It makes you protective. It makes you guarded. It makes you react to energy before it even touches you. And I had to recognize that too. Because I don't want to grow old alone. But I also refuse to be in anything that feels forced...Controlled...Manipulated... Draining...I don't want that kind of love. So, I had to learn something that didn't come easy to me: Forgiveness. Not for them. For me. Because holding on was hurting me more than anything they ever did. And this... This right here...Was the beginning of me changing my story. Not rewriting the past. But rewriting me.

Healing required me to sit alone with my thoughts and confront parts of myself I had avoided for years. Self-discovery is uncomfortable, but it is necessary. You cannot become whole until you are willing to face your truth.

Chapter 13
Healing the Mind

Healing is a journey. That's the best way I can explain it. Because healing is not something that happens overnight. It's not a switch you flip. It's not waking up one morning and suddenly feeling whole again. Healing happens in layers. Over time. Moment by moment. And sometimes. . .the smallest thing can trigger you. A memory. A smell. A song. A holiday.

Even now there are moments that still hit me deeply. Mother's Day is one of them. People assume because I'm a mother myself, that the day should feel joyful for me. And in many ways, it is. My children celebrate me. They love me. And I'm grateful for that. But there's another side to it too. A little girl inside of me still wishes she had her mother. Every year when Mother's Day approaches, I never fully know how I'm going to feel. Some years I'm okay.

Some years. . .I'm not. Because no matter how much time passes. . . there is still a space in my Heart that misses my mother. And maybe that's because there's a different kind of connection to the woman who carried you. I just know that loss leaves fingerprints. And even when life keeps moving, certain griefs stay with you. Father's Day doesn't hit me the same way. Because I adored my father. He was my protector. My safe place. But Mother's Day still carries a different kind of weight. Maybe because I never got enough time with her.

Healing teaches you something important: You can be healed...and still healing. Both can exist at the same time. As I began rebuilding my life, I slowly started returning to myself. To the things that once brought me peace. I started reading again. My aunt used to tell me that while all the other kids were outside playing...I would be curled up reading a book. And hearing that made me smile. Because without realizing it, I had started returning to my roots. Returning to me. I also found myself returning to church. Not out of routine. But because I needed healing. I needed peace. I needed something greater than myself to help carry what I couldn't carry alone. Because healing the mind...is deeper than people think. It's not just about smiling more. It's about unlearning the things that broke you quietly. Because when someone constantly tears you down, criticizes you, or makes you feel less than...you start seeing yourself through damaged eyes. Even after you leave the situation, the thoughts can remain. You still question yourself. Still wonder if you're enough. I used to be a cheerleader. Confident. Energetic. Full of life. But life changes you. Children. Stress. Trauma. Depression. And over time, your body changes too. And if I'm honest, that affected me. Because society teaches women that our worth is connected to appearance. Especially as we age. So, I had to learn this: My value was never in my size. My beauty was never attached to perfection. Healing meant learning how to see myself again with grace. Not through shame. But through love.

Real love. The kind that starts within. Healing the mind also meant giving myself permission to rest. To breathe. To stop carrying guilt for surviving. Because for so long, I survived everything… but never stopped long enough to process it. And the truth is…you cannot heal what you refuse to acknowledge.

So, I started acknowledging it. The grief. The anger. The pain. The abandonment. The insecurities. Not to stay stuck there…but to finally release it. And while I'm still healing…I'm proud of how far I've come. Because the woman I am today is no longer the little girl silently carrying everything alone. She speaks now. She feels now.

She heals now. This chapter isn't just about healing the mind. It's about giving yourself permission to become whole again. And understanding that healing doesn't mean you never hurt again. It means the hurt no longer controls your life. And that… is freedom.

Healing is not a destination; it is a lifelong journey. Certain memories and losses may never completely disappear, but they no longer have to control us. True healing happens when we learn to honor our pain without allowing it to define us.

Chapter 14
Redefining Love

For a long time, I didn't think I ever wanted to fall in love again. Not because I stopped believing love existed... but because I had experienced the wrong version of it for so long. And when pain has been attached to love long enough...you begin to fear the idea of it altogether. But healing changes your perspective. As I got older...I started realizing something important: Love is not control. Love is not fear. Love is not manipulation. And love is definitely not suffering in silence. Real love feels different. It feels safe. It feels peaceful. It feels like someone choosing you without trying to break you.

For so many years, I thought love meant endurance. Staying no matter what. Fighting no matter how tired you were. Sacrificing yourself to prove loyalty. But now I understand love differently. Love is pure. It's genuine. It's someone loving you through your flaws while still encouraging you to grow. Not tearing you down. Not humiliating you. Not making you feel small. But helping you become better. Love is support. It's encouragement.

It's being able to dream freely because the person beside you wants to see you win too. And no, love isn't perfect. I don't believe in fairy tales. Life is real. People are imperfect.

Relationships take work.

But I do believe this: Every day, two people should wake up and choose each other intentionally.

Not out of obligation. Not out of fear. Not because they feel trapped. But because love should feel mutual. And that's what I want for my children. For my grandchildren. I want them to experience healthy love. The kind of love that allows them to breathe. To grow. To feel emotionally safe. I never want them to feel forced to stay somewhere that destroys them.

And one thing I had to confront within myself was affection. Because if I'm honest...that didn't always come naturally for me.

Saying "I love you." Giving hugs. Showing softness openly. Those things were difficult sometimes. Not because I didn't love deeply...but because affection wasn't always expressed openly around me growing up. So, I had to learn it. I had to intentionally become softer.

More expressive. More emotionally available. Because I wanted my children and grandchildren to know something, I didn't always know: You are allowed to feel. You are allowed to cry. You are allowed to be vulnerable. You are allowed to express emotion without feeling weak.

Strength is not pretending nothing hurts. Real strength is allowing yourself to heal honestly.

And I pray my children experience a love that is healthy. Not toxic. Not draining. Not painful in destructive ways. Because love should never damage your spirit. And if love hurts...it should be the kind of hurt that comes from caring deeply. The hurt of letting someone go because you love them enough to stop forcing what no longer works. The hurt of losing someone through death and learning how to continue loving them through memory. That kind of love hurts...but it's still rooted in love.

And as I've healed from the loss of my parents, my grandparents and others I loved deeply...I've learned something beautiful: Love doesn't end just because someone is no longer physically here. Love remains. In memories. In lessons. In prayers. In the way they shaped you. And while I would love to still have them beside me...I also have peace knowing they are no longer suffering. That's another version of love too. Loving someone enough to let them rest.

This chapter isn't just about relationships. It's about redefining love entirely. Learning the difference between attachment and peace. Between control and care. Between surviving love and actually, feeling loved. And understanding that real love...should feel like healing, not heartbreak.

Love should never require you to lose yourself.
Through healing, I learned that genuine love is patient,
supportive, honest, and safe. The healthier I became,
the clearer my definition of love became.

Chapter 15
Finding Love Again

There was a time in my life when I truly believed love just wasn't for me anymore. Not real love, anyway. I had gone through so much emotionally, mentally, and spiritually...that I convinced myself it was safer to be alone. And honestly? I had made peace with that. I remember saying to myself, "God, maybe this just isn't in the cards for me." Because after everything I had experienced, I wasn't willing to settle anymore. I refused to go backwards. I didn't care how lonely it got. I didn't care who came along. I would rather be by myself than lose myself again.

And then life surprised me. I have a cousin more like a little brother to me and he kept talking about this coworker of his. Now one thing about him, he's protective over me. So if he was introducing me to somebody, I knew this person had to have some good qualities. Still I was hesitant. I wasn't looking for love. I wasn't trying to start over. But one day he finally convinced me. "Come meet my friend." And I remember feeling nervous. Which shocked me. Because I hadn't felt nervous about a man in a very long time. I stayed sitting in my car. Telling my cousin, "Stay out here with me." And of course...he walked off. Then he stepped out. And Lord...when I saw him...The confidence. The shoulders. That smile. The brown eyes. And for the first time in a long time...I felt something. Not pressure. Not fear. Not anxiety. Just curiosity. We talked. Simple conversation. Nothing forced. Nothing performative. And what stood out the most wasn't even his appearance. It was peace. I felt understood. And after talking to him, I realized something: We were both at a place in life where we knew what we wanted and what we didn't.

So yes...I gave him my number. Because for the first time, I could actually see potential. Not fantasy. Not survival. Potential. Then life shifted again. COVID19 happened. At the time, I was working as a manager for Rental Car Company at the airport. And when the world shuts down, everything changed. Flights stopped. Travel stopped. And eventually...I was furloughed. Then later laid off. I remember feeling uncertain. Afraid. Trying to figure out what life was going to look like next. And I'll never forget the call. He asked me, "Do you want to come over?" And truthfully...I never really left. Because over time, our connection grew naturally. Not rushed. Not forced. Just real. And what I discovered was this: Love feels completely different when it's Healthy. His hugs felt safe. His presence felt calming. His touch didn't create anxiety. It brought peace. And after years of chaos...peace felt unfamiliar. But beautiful. I loved the way he loved me.

But even deeper than that...I loved the kind of man he was. Watching him fight for his children. Show up for his children. Raise his children. That meant something to me. Because you don't always see that. And after everything I had experienced, seeing a man lead with responsibility, consistency, and love...was healing in itself. Were we perfect? No. We still have disagreements. We're human. But what we don't have is toxicity.

And that was non-negotiable for both of us. Because we both understood what unhealthy love looked like. And neither one of us wanted that anymore. So every day, we choose differently. We choose communication. We choose respect. We choose peace. And what I love most is that I can finally be myself. I don't have to walk on eggshells. I don't have to silence myself. I don't have to shrink to fit into someone else's world. I have a voice now. And even when we disagree…I'm still heard. That matters to me. More than anything. Because healthy love doesn't erase you. It allows you to bloom. And when I look back now, I realize something beautiful: I thought my story was over. I thought love had passed me by. But really… God was healing me first. Because sometimes, before God sends you the right person, He has to heal the version of you that accepted the wrong ones. And now…I'm grateful. Grateful for growth.

Grateful for peace. Grateful for second chances. And most of all… grateful that I learned love does still exist. Not the toxic version. Not the painful version. But the kind of love that feels safe, intentional, and genuine. Two imperfect people…choosing each other every single day. And honestly? That's more beautiful than any fairy tale.

After heartbreak, I never imagined I would trust love again.
Yet God showed me that healthy love feels different—it brings
peace instead of confusion. Sometimes the right person
arrives when you have finally learned your own worth.

Chapter 16
Truth Revealed

There are some truths in life that don't just shock you. They unravel you. And just when you think you've finally found peace...life will hand you something that makes you question everything you thought you knew. That's what this was for me. A truth. Hidden in plain sight. As I continued navigating life, I had finally reached a place where things felt calmer. Not perfect. But calm. Because one thing I've learned is this: Life never fully stops testing you. The problems may change. The people may change. But every season brings something new. And this season brought me...truth.

When I was little, there was a man I would refer to him as an uncle, as he was a close friend of my Mom brother. You know how families do. Everybody older becomes "uncle" or "auntie." So, to me, that's all he was. Someone connected to the family. Someone familiar. Someone safe enough to hug when he showed up at my middle school with a birthday card one year. I didn't think anything of it. I was a child. But I remember the adults reacting. Conversations happening. The card disappearing. Whispers. Then silence. Years later, after I had my daughter at fourteen, he showed up again. This time at my aunt's house. And this time...everything changed. Because he looked at me and said: "I'm your father." And I remember feeling instant anger. Confusion. Disbelief. "What are you talking about?"

Because in my mind, my father was the man who raised me. The man I cried over. The man I missed. The man I loved. So, hearing this man claim something so personal...felt offensive to me. I got upset. Hysterical. And after that, I barely saw him. But every now and then, he would appear at family gatherings. And there was always something in my spirit that became unsettled around him. I didn't understand it then. But now I realize... maybe truth has a way of stirring something in you fully understand it before your mind. Still...I ignored it. Life moved on. And so did I. Until one day...everything came crashing back.

Last year, I went to a party with my cousin the one who is more like my sister than my cousin. We were standing outside, talking, laughing,getting ourselves together...when a truck pulled up. And inside that truck...was him. The moment I saw him, something inside me shifted instantly. Anger. Tension. Emotion. Then the young woman sitting in the vehicle looked at me and said: "Is that my sister?" And in that moment...I froze. Because while she was speaking from innocence...I was reacting from years of confusion. And my response...was cold. Not because she deserved it. But because I was overwhelmed. Later that night, my cousin looked at me and said: "I've never seen you react like that before." Especially the way I treated the young woman. Because she didn't create the situation. She was simply existing inside a truth I wasn't ready to face. So the next day, I called my aunt. And I told her: "Please tell her I'm sorry." Because deep down, something in me knew this situation wasn't going away.

This happens every time as if my spirit is disturbed. That moment stayed with me. My cousin asked me the prior night during our conversation. "Why don't you just take a DNA test?" And at first, I resisted. Because sometimes. . .you avoid the truth when you know it has the power to change your entire identity. But eventually. . .I agreed. And I'll never forget that date. August 27th. I opened the email. And all I saw was: 99.9999%. And in that moment. . . my entire world shattered. I had a breakdown right there at work. Because suddenly. . . everything I thought I knew about my life felt different. This man. . . had been my biological father all along. All those years I cried over not having a living father. . . I actually did. And that realization broke something in me. Because I started replaying my entire life. Every moment I wished for a father. Every moment I felt abandoned. Every moment I wondered what it would feel like to have a dad to talk to, to lean on, to call. And all along. . .he was here. I felt betrayed. Confused. Angry. Lost. Not just because of the truth itself. . .but because other people knew.

Family knew. People carried this truth while I lived my life without it. Even my younger brother Admitted that he had heard the truth years ago. And that hurt me deeply. Because now, I didn't know who to trust anymore. My entire identity felt shaken. I remember even thinking: "Was my whole life a lie?" And what made it even harder was seeing pieces of him inside of me. Even my feet. Something I had been insecure about for years. I had gone to doctors trying to understand them, trying to "fix" them. Only to find out. . .they were genetic. And suddenly, I was staring at physical proof that this man was part of me. That realization is hard to explain. Because part of me felt relieved. Part of me felt angry. Part of me felt guilty. And part of me. . .felt numb. I wanted to thank him for never fully giving up. But emotionally. . .I still struggled to connect. My sister asked, "What was I expecting out of it"? Honestly, I thought I was missing something. And maybe that's because truth revealed late still comes with grief. Because while I gained something...I also lost something. The version of my story I had believed in my entire life. And now, I'm still learning how to process it all.

This chapter isn't just about discovering the truth. It's about identity. It's about what happens when your past suddenly changes shape. And learning that healing... sometimes means grieving the story you thought was yours.

Discovering the truth about my biological father shook
the foundation of everything I believed about my identity.
The revelation brought confusion, grief, and unanswered
questions. Yet it also taught me that truth, no matter
how painful, is often the beginning of freedom.

Chapter 17

Becoming Whole

When I sit back and really think about my life all I can say is: Wow. There were so many Moments that could have broken me completely. Moments that could have taken me out mentally, emotionally, and spiritually. And honestly, sometimes I still don't know how I made it through. But one thing I do know is this: God carried me. Even when I didn't understand Him. Even when I was angry. Even when I was making mistakes. Even when I was trying to survive instead of heal. He still carried me.

And I truly believe my parents have been watching over me too. Because when I look back over Everything I survived…I know grace covered me. Now would I have wanted my life to look different? Of course. There are choices I wish I could redo. Moments I wish I could erase. Pain, I wish I never experienced. But healing teaches you something important: You cannot rewrite the past. You can only grow from it. And that's what I've learned to do. Grow. Little by little. Day by day. Because every single morning God allows me to open my eyes...I get another chance. Another chance to choose peace. Another chance to choose healing. Another chance to become better than I was yesterday. And honestly...That's a blessing.

For so many years, I focused on everything I lost. But now...I focus on everything I still have. My children. My grandchildren. My family. My partner. My life. And when I really think about it...I'm blessed beyond measure. Not because my life was easy. But because I survived it. I'm still standing. Still breathing. Still loving. Still learning. Still becoming. And now, I want to enjoy life. Really enjoy it. I want to travel. Laugh more. Create memories. Love freely. Spend time with the people who genuinely love me.

Because for so long, I existed in survival mode. Now...I finally feel like I'm living. And there is a difference. I've learned that becoming whole doesn't mean pretending you were never broken. It means gathering every broken piece and loving yourself enough to rebuild anyway. That's what I'm doing now. Rebuilding. Pouring into myself. Protecting my peace. Choosing joy intentionally. And one of the greatest lessons I've learned is this: I am in control of me. Not my past. Not my trauma. Not other people's opinions. Not old pain. Me. That realization changed my life. Because once you understand that your healing is your responsibility... you stop waiting for someone else to save you.

You start saving yourself. Do I still mourn my parents sometimes? Absolutely. I don't think that pain ever fully leaves. You just learn how to carry it differently. Now when I think about my parents or my grandparents...I smile more. I talk to them. I thank them. I carry them with me. Especially my grandmother. My Tuga. I still feel connected to her. And those memories that once only made me cry...now bring me comfort too.

As I continue getting older, I realize I'm still discovering myself. Still peeling back layers. Still learning who I truly am outside of survival mode. And honestly...that's one of the most beautiful parts of healing. Learning to love yourself fully. Not conditionally. Not based on validation. Not based on appearance. Not based on who chooses you. But because you deserve love too. Your own love. And yes...there are still moments when I look in the mirror and critique myself. Moments where I don't feel my best. But now, anything I choose to do for myself...I do it for me. Not because someone else told me to. Not because I'm trying to prove something. But because I deserve happiness. I deserve peace. I deserve to feel whole. And that's what becoming whole means to me. Not perfection. Not pretending life didn't hurt me. But understanding my life lessons...working through them... and continuously becoming a better version of myself.

Because despite everything I've been through...I'm still here. Still healing. Still growing. Still evolving. And honestly? That's the most powerful part of my story. Not what broke me. But the fact that I found myself again.

Wholeness does not come from having a perfect life. It comes from accepting your journey, learning from your mistakes, and choosing growth over regret. I am no longer defined by what happened to me—I am defined by how I responded to it.

Chapter 18

Evolving Into Peace

Writing this story was not easy for me. For years, I carried these thoughts inside of me. Quietly. Privately. Painfully. I would write little pieces here and there, journal my emotions, replay memories in my mind...but I could never fully get past the pain of losing my parents and my grandmother. That kind of loss leaves a hole. A deep one. And honestly...some grief never fully disappears. You simply learn how to carry it. But this time... I finished the story. I told it. Not because it was easy. But because it was time. Time for my voice to be heard. Time for my children and grandchildren to understand me more deeply. Because throughout life, they saw different versions of me. The hurt version. The angry version. The surviving version. The growing version. But at the core of it all...I'm just an imperfect woman who has been through a lot.

A woman still learning. Still healing. Still evolving. And yes, some things that happened in my childhood were completely beyond my control.

I was just a little girl. But as I got older, I also had to accept another truth: Some of the roads I went down came from my own choices too. And healing requires honesty. Not blame. Not excuses. Honesty. Because accountability is part of growth. And while I can acknowledge my pain, I refuse to stay stuck in it. I cannot live my life wallowing in everything that hurt me. So every day...I pick myself up. Dust myself off. And keep moving forward. Do I still wonder how different my life may have been if my parents had lived? Absolutely. Especially my dad. Because he believed in me. He supported me. Loved me loudly. And I often wonder what my life would have looked like with that continued guidance. But I also recognize that God still placed people in my life to help shape me. My aunts who took me in. The family members who poured into me. The people who corrected me. Guided me. Prayed for me. Even the people who hurt me. Because every single person played a role in my story.

Every lesson taught me something. And one thing I know now is this: If you don't learn from your lessons...you will repeat them. That is why breaking cycles matter so much to me. Not just for myself...but for my children and my grandchildren. I want them to recognize unhealthy patterns sooner. I want them to make wiser decisions. I want them to know they deserve peace, love, and emotional safety.

Will they still make mistakes? Of course. Because nobody is perfect. I still make mistakes too. But every morning we wake up, God gives us another opportunity to try again. Another chance to grow. Another chance to become better than we were yesterday. And that is grace. This story was never written to bash anyone. It was never about exposing every dark detail.

Because honestly...everything wasn't even told. Some things remain between me and God. But this story was about truth. Accountability. Healing. Clarity. Closure. And hopefully...purpose.

Because if my story can help somebody else feel less alone...then every tear it took to write this was worth it. I want you to understand that healing is possible. That cycles can be broken. That your past does not have to define your future.

And most importantly...that peace matters. More than money. More than appearances. More than proving a point. Peace is priceless. And now, that's what I protect the most. My peace. My joy. My healing.

I want to laugh more. Smile more. Travel more. Love deeper. Be present. Enjoy my family. Enjoy my grandchildren. Create memories. Because life is too short to spend it carrying unnecessary heaviness. Will every day be perfect? No. But every day is still a gift. And one of the biggest blessings in my life are the relationship I now have with my children. That matters to me deeply. Because when it's all said and done, legacy matters. Not perfection. Legacy. I want the people I love to remember me with warmth. With laughter. With love. I want my name to bring smiles to their faces. Because I am evolving. Still evolving. Like a butterfly. And if there's one thing I hope you take from my story, it's this: You are not disqualified because life hurt you. You are not broken beyond repair. You are allowed to grow. Allowed to heal. Allowed to begin again. No matter how many chapters your life has already written. Because becoming whole isn't about having a perfect story. It's about finding peace within your imperfect one.

The greatest gift I have found in this season of life is peace. Not perfection. Not validation. Peace. Every lesson, heartbreak, and victory brought me to this place of understanding that true happiness begins when you choose yourself and protect your peace.

Epilogue
Choosing Me

If there's one thing I've learned through this journey called life... it's that life will stretch you. It will break you. It will humble you. But it will also grow you. And when I look back over my life now, I can honestly say...it wasn't easy. There were so many ups and downs. So many moments where I felt lost. Moments where I questioned myself. Moments where I wondered, "How did I even survive that?" But mixed in with all of that pain...were beautiful moments too. Moments of laughter. Moments of love. Moments of grace. Moments that reminded me life was still worth living.

And today, I'm grateful for all of it. Even the hard parts. Because without those trials, I would not be the woman I am today. Those experiences shaped me. They strengthened me. They taught me. And even the things that once felt negative...I can now see differently. Because pain has a way of teaching you what truly matters. I no longer take life for granted. I no longer take peace for granted. I no longer take waking up each morning for granted. Every day above ground is a blessing to me now. And these days,I'm simply enjoying life. Enjoying my children. My grandchildren. My partner. His children. My family. Just enjoying love, connection, and presence. Because at one point in my life, I was surviving so hard that I forgot how to simply live. Now...I live intentionally. Now don't get me wrong...life still isn't perfect. I still face challenges. Even with my adult children, there are moments that test me. But one thing I know now is this: That too shall pass. And that mindset alone has carried me through so much.

If there's anything I want my readers to take from my story, it's this: Do not allow anyone to put you in a box. Do not allow anyone to shame you for your past. Do not allow anyone to diminish your character because of mistakes you made while trying to survive life. Your past does not define you. Your mistakes do not define you. Your trauma does not define you. What defines you is who you choose to become every single day you wake up.

That's where your power is. And I want you to know something: You are loved. Even if nobody around you says it...you say it to yourself. You encourage yourself. You motivate yourself. You pour into yourself. Because self-love matters. And every decision you make in life...make sure it's something that genuinely brings you peace. Not because somebody else wanted it for you. Not because society told you to. Not because you're trying to prove something. But because it makes you happy.

That's the journey I'm on now. A journey of peace. A journey of choosing me. And one thing I've learned is this: It's never too late to redirect your life. No, I didn't end up in the medical field like I once dreamed. But that's okay. Life took me in another direction. I earned my bachelor's degree in Criminal Justice with a minor in Corrections and Case Management

Today, I work as an Administrative Professional. And honestly? I enjoy what I do. But the beautiful thing about life is this: As long as God wakes me up, I still have choices. I can still evolve. I can still dream. I can still become. And that realization is freeing. Because now, I no longer live my life based on fear, guilt, or survival.

I live my life from a place of peace. And after everything I've been through…that peace means everything to me. Because at the end of the day, the greatest relationship I've built wasn't with another person. It was with me. And finally…I can honestly say: I love me. And that changes everything.

My story is proof that your beginning does not determine your ending. No matter what you have endured, you can heal, grow, and create a life filled with purpose and peace. The greatest transformation of my life happened when I finally chose to love, value, and believe in myself.

The End.

www.ingramcontent.com/pod-product-compliance
Lightning Source LLC
LaVergne TN
LVHW090106250926
848814LV00049B/50/J
* 9 7 9 8 2 3 4 0 8 9 5 1 9 *